THE BONES POEMS

The Bones Poems

William Virgil Davis

Copyright © 2014 by William Virgil Davis
All Rights Reserved

ISBN: 978-0-9911074-6-9
Library of Congress Control Number: 2014937759
Manufactured in the United States of America
Book Design: Heather Odom

Lamar University Press
Beaumont, TX

for

Carol

Bill and Jean

Sarah and Caroline

bones of my bones

Poetry from Lamar University Press

Alan Berecka, *With Our Baggage*
David Bowles, *Flower, Song, Dance*: Aztec *and Mayan Poetry* (a new translation)
Jerry Bradley, *Crownfeathers and Effigies*
Jeffrey DeLotto, *Voices Writ in Sand*
Mimi Ferebee, *Wildfires and Atmospheric Memories*
Ken Hada, *Margaritas and Redfish*
Michelle Hartman, *Disenchanted and Disgruntled*
Lynn Hoggard, *Motherland, Stories and Poems from Louisiana*
Gretchen Johnson, *A Trip Through Downer, Minnesota*
Janet McCann, *The Crone at the Casino*
Erin Murphy, *Ancilla*
Dave Oliphant, *The Pilgrimage, Selected Poems: 1962-2012*
Carol Reposa, *Underground Musicians*
Carol Smallwood, *Water, Earth, Air, Fire, and Picket Fences*

www.LamarUniversityPress.Org

Poetry by William Virgil Davis

Landscape and Journey.
Winter Light.
The Dark Hours.
One Way to Reconstruct the Scene.

I wonder, have I lived a skeleton's life,
As a disbeliever in reality,

A countryman of all the bones in the world?

—Wallace Stevens

Acknowledgments

These skeletal constructions are here preserved from earlier existences. Many of them have had long lives and most of them have already appeared clothed in various forms and disguises, but I have patched and pieced them together again here in new configurations.

I am pleased to acknowledge the places where they first stepped forth:

Artful Dodge
Arts in Society
Calliope
The Carleton Miscellany
Circus Maximus
The Chariton Review
The Dark Hours
Grasslands Review
Gray Sky Review
Grub Street
The Hampden-Sydney Poetry Review
Images
One Way to Reconstruct the Scene
The Pawn Review
Pembroke Magazine
Perspective
Poem
Poet Lore
Poetry Northwest
Prairie Schooner
Shenandoah
Slackwater Review
The Southern Poetry Review
The University of Windsor Review

CONTENTS

1   Proem
2   After Centuries
4   Again
6   Their Arrival
9   The Bones Meet the Bones
10   Their Dance
11   In the Pit
12   The Bones Die and Go On Living
15   Following the Bones
16   The Recognition
17   They Bend Bunched Together
18   Their Odyssey
21   The Bones Circle
22   They Bend Above Water
23   The Drowned
24   In the Dark
25   The Holes
26   On a Binge
27   They Make Love
28   The Anniversarȳ
30   After Three Days
31   They Gather Together
32   Trespass
33   Meeting the Bones
35   Where the Bones Move
38   Their Sleep
39   The Metamorphosis
40   When the Hand from the Dark
41   Another Meeting
42   After Dark

45	Murderers
46	Some Things the Bones Never Know
47	The Séance
49	The Bones in Search of a Bed
50	Renting Your Bed to the Bones
51	Their Words
52	They Have Risen
53	In the Museum
54	The Way
55	The Closet
57	The Bones Come Home
60	After Words
61	In Far Fields
62	Their Dance
63	Their Death
64	Their Death and Life
65	Oil
66	They Shiver
67	The Promise
68	And If Shriven at Last They Rise
69	Their Light
70	They Come Close They Disappear
71	Not Many Years
72	Their Departure
74	Gone
75	Into the Dark
76	Growing Darker as They Deepen
77	At the Cemetery
78	At Rest

Proem

they begin their journey back to flesh

they stand alone in the wind
and the wind
clothes them with words
and the words
break out on the silence
as if reborn

to speak to those who are still in their skins

After Centuries

after centuries
the arms
have come free

they put their hands
to their heads
find the tucked-in end

and begin

to unwind
the bindings

they loosen
some of the bandages
then rest

stretch

relax

they stand
near a door

white light
as fine as dust

seeps

under the door

puddles
beneath their feet

Again

disembodied
they dig through heaps
of themselves

here a severed arm
there a foot
fingers and thumbs

cracked kneecaps
crushed skulls
broken ribs

they assemble
themselves
as best they can

next they need
clothes bushels
of clothes lie around

every size color
brand-new worn
they try them on

one after another
find a comfortable
fit stand step up

through earth to air

Their Arrival

they come
old and young
one from east of the wind
with a burlap
bag on his back
and his head
hung down
on his chest

another
from west of the moon
with a long
white beard
and a lightning scar
across his arm
and a lame leg
so old
so used to the dark
he has lost his shadow

three or four
arrive at night
creep into camp
and fall
asleep
in a heap
by the fire

two come
together arm
in arm
holding
each other up
one bottle between them
stumbling in
as much on instinct
as memory

for hours
days
weeks
months
who knows how many
years
too numerous to name
they arrive
in hordes
herds
flocks
some straggling in
alone
or two or three
at a time

coming
from under stones
stepping out
of trees

rising up
from rushing waters
with every waft
of wind
so many
so various
too many to name

they come
as if
to begin
again

The Bones Meet the Bones

under cover of dark
the bones move between the trees
step silently
over twigs
stones

walk on water in the long
moonlight

no one would know they were there

then
from the other direction
coming toward them as inevitably
as death

the bones come striding

alert in the moonlight
as clean as rain

bones meet bones in a small meadow

they walk up to one another like old friends
and fall on each other's shoulders
and weep so loudly

even the wind stops to listen

Their Dance

they step up
out
on air
on silence
in the wind's abrasive embrace

they begin to sway with the wind
bending their backs
back
remembering rhythm

they improvise as they go
their feet charting the dark
moving to music
they only half-remember

all night long
they dance
the wind
and their own rhythm
warming them

In the Pit

in the pit
in the deep dark
where there is no light
where even the wind whispers
and only the oldest stones
dare speak
blind worms
move slowly over the bones
and create
with their intricate embroidery
a moving tapestry
the model of a mind
articulately arranged

The Bones Die and Go On Living

death was so strong
it made them vomit

then they fell asleep

an underground wind blew through them
chilling them
they shuddered in their sleep

they didn't know about death

when they awoke
freed of the flesh
of the thin sack of skin surrounding them
of the stale smell of dried sweat

they didn't know where they were

a chill morning wind
burned through them
and they
shuddered again

the sun began to burn
warming the water
warming the stones

they took a deep breath
and sat up

adjusted their empty eyesockets
to the dim light
and looked around with wonder

they stretched
they struggled to stand

then they began to understand

they stepped up
out of the hole
took one tentative step
or two

they walked
they ran

once or twice they fell
they picked themselves up

they were so happy they could not contain themselves

when they couldn't find
their shadows
they knew they were invisible

they laughed out loud
they answered their own hollow echo

in the years that followed
the bones
had many adventures

some of them will be remembered forever

some are written down here

Following the Bones

the bones do not remember the soft skin
that surrounded them

they pull the dark blood from the skin
and stand up on their own

they walk in the shapes of shadows
and shine in the dark wind

you have followed them
even though you do not know where they are going

The Recognition

when they bend
close

to the earth

their shadows
fill

with flesh

They Bend Bunched Together

they bend bunched together
as if to keep warm

the wind sings through them
and the flames flame through

after it is over
they each go off in their own directions

Their Odyssey

three days without water
or shelter
with only the stale wind
for companion

they begin slowly
to move forward again
sand spilling
from holes in their skulls
blowing through their ribcages
grating in crevices
of knees
and elbows

every step
a strain

even at night
they burn in the burnt black wind

but still
they move
leaving no footprints
alone and lonely
the sand
as wide as their eyes
extend

on the fourth day
they fall

then they begin to crawl
blinded
by sun and sand

mirages
appear in thin air

they smile
and hurry ahead

on the sixth day
living by now
on sweat alone
they drag themselves
over the sand
their breath
halting out

at night
against their will
they roll themselves up in a ball
and fall asleep

tongues of wind
whistle above them
and through them

before morning
almost fully covered with sand
they dig down deeper
seeking sleep
some end
to their ordeal

suddenly
the wind stops

the hush
loud

they stir
stand
begin to move forward again

each step an ache

they totter
they almost fall
move slowly

something they see

in new light
they drink
the dark
away

The Bones Circle

the bones circle
sniff
the damp earth

they seem to decide it will do
and turn

to step into the hole

They Bend Above Water

they bend
above water
drink
back death

see themselves
staring
at them there

they hesitate

as if to think
it all over

satisfied

they smile
cup their hands
and drink

The Drowned

like an image in a mirror
misted over
they sink from sight

falling through water
deeper than dreams
pulling their long screams

down with them

In the Dark

they root in the dark
send out feelers

find soft damp places
where water waits

where thin strings of light
penetrate

they begin to grow

move darkly
up their own dark veins

like vines
alive

seeking sunlight
and life

even though life
was what they died of

The Holes

they find holes
in the wind and walk through them

doors in the dark open

they move deeper down
the wind among them

whispering
whispering

what they will never hear

On a Binge

they are drunk again

one bottle between them
they walked off with the wind

just around the bend in an old road

they sat down together
to finish it off

they fell asleep right there

where anyone
who happened to come along

could fall or trip into them

They Make Love

they are stripping off skin
letting it fall to the floor

naked
they switch
the lights off
and clash
in the dark
like armies

all night long
the sparks fly up
from them
burn away
in the wind

it is as exciting as death

The Anniversary

awake before midnight
they open their eyes
uncross their arms

awaiting
what is to come

at first
nothing

they lie still
strain
to hear

faint wind
close to the earth

then louder
more distinct

the even beat of feet

they pretend to be asleep

the heavy weight
of earth
spins off

the warm night air
rushes in

they squint
and take a deep breath

and begin to unbend

then
before it begins again
it is over

light and wind
are taken away
loose earth
falls to fill in
the hole

they hold their breath
as long as they can

After Three Days

after three days without water or shelter
alone on the empty sand
with only the stale wind for companion

when anyone else would have given up

the bones grit their teeth
spit at death
and drink away the dark

They Gather Together

those that were broken by life
are made whole

those who lost limbs
have their limbs restored

those born deformed
remain deformed

but no one speaks of it

they gather together in the early light of morning

they begin marching
move in turn with a silent song

they gain momentum

they maneuver to let the others in
amending their ranks
as they go

they are singing
their ranks swelling with their music

Trespass

if you step in the bones shadow
even though they are still asleep

they stir awaken and rise
as if from death

they bless you your trespass
put their arms around you
cold cold
kiss you

and your body begins to burn as if with desire

and when you go off with them
there is only the one shadow

and the bones the bones are still asleep

Meeting the Bones

the bones are drunk again
as night falls as shadows
step into shadows and the bells
in the old church tower announce
midnight you hear them coming
before you see them they stop
to rest every few feet
fall against lampposts trip
over curbs moving slowly
into view they lurch
down the dimly-lighted street
in search of sleep

just as you are about to collide
they step aside to let you pass

the next thing you know
you awaken behind a row of bushes
not far from a small circle
of light at the edge
of a park a policeman
stands over you his flashlight
bent to your face the faint
fall of a fountain overflowing
in the distance he bends
down to test your breath and asks
you your name and where you live
he asks you what happened

you fix your face in a smile
and tell him you don't remember
the bones inside you are laughing

Where the Bones Move

when you move
your bones move
below you
under the earth
stalking
the footprints
of your shadow

as if you were walking
on water
your form
reflecting
beneath the water
head down
in the dark
currents
where the bones move

when you bend
close
to the earth
putting your ear
near your ear
your heads together
your feet treading
water and air
you hear
the dark words

seep
from your skull
grow
upward beneath you
lodge
in your mind

as you walk
you listen

you speak to hear

then
listen again

you run
following the bones

they run
following you

you are old friends and enemies

it has been
too long
since you have seen
one another

since
you have sat down
together
and talked

in the dark hours

Their Sleep

when you sleep
they walk out in the dark

all night
restless

they hike hills
wade rivers
flame in the wind

with dawn
they turn and return to your bed
take up your skin
and step off again

muffled

invisible

The Metamorphosis

you feel yourself
going over to them

your hands
are like hands

your feet
remember to move forward

your breath spills
to your chest

blows back
in your face in even rhythm

still

you know

they mimic you

these bones
you have slept in

since long before you were born

When the Hand from the Dark

when the hand from the dark waves
the bones rise up
and gather together

they march the dark morning
moving quietly through
the long grass

going back to the dark

they whisper together
and laugh

all night unable to sleep
you hear them moving
marching

you hear their inaudible laughter

Another Meeting

they get everywhere before you

when you arrive
they step out to meet you

stretch forth their hands to greet you
like an old friend

come home

After Dark

at night
as you enter your dream
the bones get up from your bed
to take their exercise

they step from the bedside
walk out
through the wall

they jump the garden fence
and whistle away

creatures of habit
and necessity
they keep to the alleys
taking their usual walks
following their typical tracks

they take a few turns
around a long block
moving like shadows
through dark alleys
behind houses

dogs tied up to watch
and give warning
do not bark
they know them
by sight and smell

the bones feed them
and the dogs lie down again
go back to sleep
on their paws

they walk
to the edge of town
and out of town

they travel dirt roads
no one sees
how they gleam
in the dim moonlight

they always stop
at the cemetery
for an hour or two

then
before morning
when the first faint light
brushes the sky
and their shadows
fall in front of them
they turn to return

they follow the same routes
summer and winter
in spite of the weather

at last they climb in
through the window again
step to the side
of the bed and lie back down
with you
shaping their shapes
to the shape you are sleeping in
and if you are dreaming
they dream
your dream with you

you have never known
them not to return
not to be there
to greet you

when you awaken

Murderers

they stalk you in the dark

each time you turn
they disappear
or lie as still as stones

when you begin again
they reassemble themselves
take up your footprints
and follow

stopping when you stop
moving forward when you move forward

Some Things the Bones Never Know

when you sleep
they think you have died

when you awaken
they believe in miracles

when you hide
they look for you

when you die
they are born to the air

they say
where did he go

The Séance

they are ushered into a room
and directed to take a chair
the room is small and square

they are told to hold hands
told to close their eyes

the music begins
the table starts to rise

a bright white light
like a crystal globe frosted
with shadowy smoke
fills the small room
is focused
on the curtain in front of them

they feel a draft
the curtain begins to blow softly
in an invisible breeze
a voice speaks almost audibly

words are repeated
again and again

they are told to keep their eyes
closed
told they will be given
further directions

their hands are cold
slimy with sweat
their knees knock
music ebbs and flows
like something seeping up
from somewhere underground

suddenly it stops

curtains quiver and part

they are told to open their eyes

before them on a small platform
half-hidden
no more than a shelf protruding from a wall
stands a living man
fully clothed in flesh

he beckons to them

they fall back in a faint
their eyes

wide

wild

The Bones in Search of a Bed

a hand comes up the banister
outside the bedroom door
they hesitate
the wind hushes
under the door
and the angle of light
opens slowly

you slide over the side
of the bed
and pull yourself in
under it

the bones
stop beside the side
of the bed and the bed
takes their weight
like a shadow disappearing
into dark

they stretch out above you
adjusting their shapes
to the shape you made
in the sheets

beneath them on the dusty floor
you fall asleep
in the empty sack of your skin

Renting Your Bed to the Bones

you have rented your bed
to the bones
they came saying they needed
a place to sleep
all night you dug in the dark
working your way around stones
pulling up roots of trees
clearing the plot
at last the earth opened
like water
when the hole was wide enough
and deep breathing
evenly in the dark air
the bones stepped
into it like owners
and lay down
they shifted their weight
slightly to find
a comfortable rest and then
fell asleep you covered
them over with the soft earth
and left the rent
will not be due for years

Their Words

their words
keep

composing

decomposing

the names
of your name

They Have Risen

they have risen with your shadow
and stepped forth
stretching the old skin

tight around themselves
and gone off
wherever you led

when they hid
in the dark
you waited up for them

when they returned your shadow
you slept
together again

In the Museum

dry air
bodies the bones

they stand and stare

you stare
back at them

The Way

you have felt them
sigh

and answered them

bent your back
back

your fingers
tight
on the web of your hand

turned toes
beneath
your feet

walked with them

knowing
they knew

the way

The Closet

you open a door
and find them there
hung on a hook

their parts labeled
with labels
marked with inks
and arrows a few
of them bent
out of shape

back together
out of place
bits broken off
the whole strung
together on wires

swaying there
in the dark

you stare at them
they stare at you

what can
you do

you take them
into your arms

like old friends forgotten
surprised to be found
again

you put your arms
around them
they their arms around you
your flesh

caught

as if in a vise

The Bones Come Home

for more than a mile
the bones
like a basket of junk continually collapsing
have been following you

you tried hiding in doorways
running down darkened alleys
cutting across lawns

they stop when you stop
move when you move
their awkward gait
insistent
not to be denied

at home at last
you enter the darkened rooms
step out of your shadow
and begin to climb the stairs

you hear them stop outside the door
hear the door open

the night air come in with them

at the top of the stairs
you turn and see them standing there
below you
just beyond the landing
balanced against the banister
waiting for you to turn
to continue

when you get to your own room
you station yourself
behind the door
and wait

you hear them stop at the top of the stairs
to catch their breath

then
breathing evenly again
they make their way along the long hall

they enter your room and
hesitate
as if they needed time
to adjust to the dimmed light

then they step to the side of your bed
standing between you

and the light
which shines straight through them

their empty eyesockets
fill with fire

your eyes begin to burn

After Words

the bones step out of their dark cave of body

they burn in the wind

they blow away with the wind

the wind has taken their speech away

there is nothing left to say

In Far Fields

in fields far from home
the bones are eating rain

free of the flesh
they rest in damp earth

as the sounds of life die out
as they dream their favorite dream

they have already forgotten your name

Their Dance

the skin peels off
falls like old
wallpaper

at last
they are born

they lift themselves
to dance
their ribs remembering

to rise and fall

they never want
to lie down again

Their Death

they never die

Their Death and Life

their body fell through them
like dust

even when burned it was not
death

the dust blew away
in the wind

the wind rose
found water

fell
through damp earth

warmed them
to growth again

Oil

they add like oil
loose their own designs

fall into heaps

the heaps begin to grow

they dare the wind
to stop speaking of them

They Shiver

they shiver
rubbing together

this deep in dark
no sound
but water running

they
pool their energies

burning

to begin again

The Promise

and if one day they will rise
do not let the light know
or the ground which covers them
which was always warm
or even this song they sang
this sad long song no
do not let it know

let it come if it comes
like unexpected water when roots
are dry like lightning
in a calm summer sky
or animals new-born stepping out
on new-fallen snow or
breath where no lungs are

And If Shriven at Last They Rise

and if shriven at last they rise
and their parts report as promised
and fly through the air
to sing like some winged instrument

then let it be like the breath
they took and gave in life
like the rivers of air they drank
or the death they died to

without pain or pause
unnoticed until it was over

Their Light

they drink a cup of darkness
like water
like breath taken in

they sing their song
in the dark caves of the body

when you have forgotten them
they stand upright in the wind

and the wind is like long music
and the dark

and the dark
has never been so bright

They Come Close They Disappear

twilight
the sky run together
like watercolor
like a final startle of birds

they sway away on the road
the road that runs on forever

their arms around one another
their laughter broken like bricks

they never turn or look back
they never stop talking and singing

when one of them stumbles
and falls the others keep going

the road is longer than they remember
they move before them and follow

they come close they disappear

Not Many Years

not many years from now
when they dig through the debris
they will find a stone
among the bones
and not knowing what
they are looking for
or finding have found
they will throw it away
never realizing
how deep the bones dug
to find the stone
never stopping to listen
to what it is whispering
or see when they smash it
how the light
splinters

Their Departure

and then one morning
before morning
the dew still heavy in grass

even before birds

slowly
they rise
yawning
covered with frost

as if new
or newly born

their joints creak and crack in the wind

silently
they step together

quietly
take their places

speaking softly

they stand
beautiful in the sunlight
fingering them

turning them golden

in the wind
blown through them

slowly
they walk off
together

two by two

into still darkened distance
singing as they go

not yet out of sight
dancing
the line of them moving
dancing
as far as the eye can see

in no more than a moment
they are gone

without even an echo

and the air
is empty again

and the day
dawned

Gone

they sway away
down a dusty road
their arms locked together

they do not
turn or look back

if one of them
falls
they seem not to notice

they know the road
is as long as they are

Into the Dark

like shadows
within shadows
they glide
from tree to tree
moving off
always
ahead of you

then they glance
back
and smile
their teeth
gleaming
in the moonlight

they turn
step off again

beckon

you follow them

moving further
and further

into the dark

Growing Darker as They Deepen

growing darker as they deepen
like water seeping
through holes only worms
could find

they twist and turn

and if at last they rise
like water sprung from rock
or water sprung from water
they rise the way they were

from shadow into shadow
as silently as skin
grafts on to skin or bone to bone

dying to be born again

At the Cemetery

the site selected at random
no one knew they were there

air like water fell
to fill the hole
the shovels sharp
against them
struck sparks
they didn't scream

the living men
stopped to stare

and then they put
this other in and covered
them all over again

At Rest

now the bones are at rest
no one need know where they've gone
or what they dream to do

the bones are at rest content

perhaps they are dead
perhaps they are only asleep

no doubt they will never return
to haunt your dreams as they have

for now anyhow it is over
this endless emptying
this filling

so much like what we name breath

www.ingramcontent.com/pod-product-compliance
Lightning Source LLC
Chambersburg PA
CBHW020949090426
42736CB00010B/1331